To: Gary
Happy Birthday

From: Mommy   Oct 26/88

Published by
GRANDREAMS LIMITED
Jadwin House, 205/211 Kentish Town Road,
London NW5.

Printed in Rumania

JB3-4   ISBN 0 86227 425 7

1

Tall Tales

Horseflies are so big in Montana that cowboys don't
swat them; they lasso them, saddle them, and ride
them.

There's a place in Africa where the mice grow so big
that the only thing they're afraid of are elephants.

Some brands of Mexican chilli peppers are so hot that
only fire-eaters are allowed to eat them.

There's a sultan who's so rich that he hires millionaires
to shine his shoes.

I knew a boy who was so unlucky that black cats
wouldn't cross his path.

There's a dog in Hollywood who's so smart that he not
only speaks, but also recites poetry.

In the South Seas, the oysters are so big that the
natives use pearls as bowling balls.

There's an apartment house so tall that in order to
reach the penthouse, you have to take a rocket.

A man in London has so many credit cards that he
and his wife use them to play poker.

The traffic in London is so bad that cockroaches on
skateboards get across town faster than taxis do.

There's an intersection in Paris that's so busy and
confusing, they hired an octopus to direct traffic.

The soil in parts of Wales is so rocky that the
worms have to carry little jack hammers.

Then there was the comedian who was so bad that his
jokes couldn't even make a hyena laugh.

There's a pet Beagle in New Jersey who's so smart, he
teaches his master tricks.

There's a joke so funny that no one can tell it because
when people hear it, they die laughing.

One lady in London was so thick that she cut a hole in
her umbrella so she could tell when the rain
stopped.

Jets are so big now that the first time pilots fly them,
they have to put stabilizers on the planes.

In Alaska, the fireflies are so big that if you catch
them in your bare hands, you get a shock.

2

There's a hotel in London that's so tall, the lift operator has to have a pilot's licence.

There's a bald eagle in the Far West who's so self conscious that he never appears in public without wearing a hat.

A rich society couple owned a canary who was so sophisticated that it wouldn't sing unless it was accompanied by a symphony orchestra.

Hailstorms are so bad in the Far North that if you stick three hailstones together, you've got a snowman.

There's a guy so lazy that he traded in his Beagle for a Great Dane so he wouldn't have to bend over to stroke his dog.

There's a place in Scotland where the flies are so big that people have to use tennis rackets to swat them.

There's a vegetable farmer in Sussex who's so big that he makes the Green Giant look like a leprechaun.

Bullfrogs grow so big in Texas that they have to wear rings in their noses.

There was a leopard who was such a meticulous dresser that he used to take baths in spot remover.

There's a building in New York City that's so tall, water has to take vitamins before it can run up to the top floor.

In Essex, they grow water melons so big that they hollow out the insides, put wheels on them, and sell them as caravans.

There's a place at the North Pole that's so cold at night, the people have to huddle around their refrigerators to keep warm.

There was a pole vaulter in the 1968 Olympics who vaulted himself so high that they're still waiting for him to come down.

And of course there was the squirrel who was so absent minded that he had to draw himself a map every time he buried a nut.

There's a mansion so big in Hertfordshire that the owner has to hire a taxi to drive him from his bedroom to the kitchen.

I knew a boy who had a fever so high that anyone who sat too close to him got sunburn.

There is a computer today that is so complicated it takes another computer to run it.

Hollywood's biggest star gets so much mail that he opened his own post office.

A mattress company has just introduced a new
  mattress that's so firm, people bruise their knees
  on it when they climb into bed.

The trees in California are so tall that the squirrels
  have to wear oxygen masks when they collect nuts.

There is a shirt fabric now that is so advanced, it
  washes and irons itself while you are sleeping.

A man in London owns a top hat so tall he has to walk
  on his knees when he goes through door ways.

There is a gift shop owner in Surrey who went into
  shock after the Christmas holidays when nobody
  came in to exchange anything.

There is an actress in Hollywood who's won so many
  Academy Awards, she rents them out to other
  actresses as pets.

A windmill in Holland got to spinning so fast one day
  that it took off and landed 45 minutes later in
  Belgium.

There's a new car on the market that's so economical, it
  uses an old salad cream jar for a petrol tank.

The thin man in the circus was so thin, he had to stop
  playing "Fetch" with his dog because the dog
  always brought *him* back instead of the stick.

A woman in Kensington has such large eyes that when
  she winks, the wind from her eyelids blows out a
  burning match.

A student at Southside School is so thin that when he
  stands sideways, the teacher marks him absent.

Nuclear submarines are now so long that it takes two
  captains to command them — one at each end.

A farm in Hampshire is so big that when the young
  couples go out to milk the cows, their
  grandchildren bring back the milk.

A woman in Hull was such an eager housekeeper that
  she scrubbed the floors of her home until she fell
  through to the basement.

The fog in London is so thick that they use it to stuff
  pillows. By pouring ink on it and chopping it up,
  they can even sell it for coal.

A farmer's daughter has such bright red hair that when
  she leaves the house before sunrise, the cocks begin
  to crow.

Snowflakes fall so large in Aberdeen that parasol
  makers merely have to stick handles in them.

Laugh Time

The new bank clerk was given a package of 5 pound notes with the instructions to count them and see if there were a hundred.

He counted up to fifty-eight and then threw the bundle down.

"*Why did you stop?*" *asked the bank manager.*

"If it's right this far," said the clerk, "it's probably right all the way."

Landlady (to New Boarder): An inventor once had this room. He invented an explosive.
New Boarder: Oh, I suppose those spots on the ceiling are the explosive.
Landlady: No, that's the inventor.

Jim: Boy, I wish I had enough money to buy an elephant!
Slim: Whatever do you want an elephant for?
Jim: I don't. I just wish I had that much money.

Plumber: I'm sorry I'm late, but I just couldn't get here any sooner.
Man of the House: Well, time hasn't been wasted. While we were waiting for you, I taught my wife how to swim.

Sarge: How long can you use a tea-bag?
Marge: Indefinitely, as long as you keep using rusty water.

Myrtle: Gosh, Mabel, what have you done to your hair? It looks like a wig!
Mabel: It is a wig!
Myrtle: Goodness, you'd never know it!

Hughie: A funny thing happened to me today. I was at the racetrack and bent over to tie my shoe, when some shortsighted jockey strapped a saddle on my back.
Louie: *Astonishing! What did you do?*
Hughie: What could I do? I ran the best race I could and came in third.

"Pardon me, sir, but do you know the way to the post office?"
"No, I'm afraid I don't."
"Well, it's two blocks up this street and three blocks to the right."

Shop Assistant: What do you want for 50 pence — the earth with a whitewashed fence around it?
Little Girl: Let me see it, please.

Small Sam was gazing into the crib at his new baby sister, who lay wailing at the top of her voice.
"Has she just come from heaven?" inquired Small Sam tenderly.
"Yes," replied his mother.
"Well," said Small Sam, "it's no wonder they put her out."

Ted: What's the best way to avoid falling hair?
Ned: Jump out of the way.

Randy: I can be sick for nothing because my father's a doctor.
Sandy: That's nothing. I can be good for nothing because my father's a minister.

PTA Mother (to Guest Speaker): Do you believe in clubs for teenagers?
Guest Speaker: Only if kindness fails.

Ann: I'm saving my money to buy one of those small Japanese radios.
Nan: How are you going to understand what they're saying?

"Do you like Duncan Hines?
"Don't know. Never dunked any."

Mother: There were two slices of pie in the cupboard this morning and now there is only one. Can you explain that?
Small Sam: *It was so dark, I didn't see the other piece.*

Fresh Frank was given an orange by a lady visitor.
"What do you say to the nice lady?" his mother prompted.
Fresh Frank replied, "Peel it."

Sy: I've invented something that will allow people to see through walls.
Hy: *Wonderful, what do you call it?*
Sy: A window.

The elevator to success runs so seldom, it's best to take the stairs.

Customer: What do you do with the leftover holes in your doughnuts?
Baker: *We tie them up with string and make fish nets out of them.*

Once upon a time a man invented a product that would grow hair on a snooker ball. He died in poverty though, because nobody wanted to buy a snooker ball with hair on it.

"Why don't you answer the phone?"
"Because it isn't ringing."
"Must you always wait till the last minute?"

Herbert: What would you like to drink?
Helen: *Ginger Ale.*
Herbert: Pale?
Helen: *Oh, no. A glassful will be sufficient.*

"Isn't that little thing too small to be a watchdog?"
"Well, he's a wrist-watchdog."

7

Policeman: Didn't you hear me yell for you to stop?
Motorist: No, I didn't.
Policeman: Didn't you see me signal for you to stop?
Motorist: No, I didn't.
Policeman: Didn't you hear me blow my whistle for you to stop?
Motorist: No, I didn't.
Policeman: Well, I guess I might as well go home. I don't seem to be doing much good around here.

Boss: If Mr. Simmons comes in to see me today, tell him I'm out.
Receptionist: Yes, sir.
Boss: And don't let him catch you doing any work, or he won't believe you.

Once upon a time there was a rich man who owned four Rolls Royces — one for each direction.

"Statistics say that a man is hit by a speeding car every four minutes."
"Poor fellow!"

Foreman: Why do you only carry one board at a time? All the other workers carry two.
Worker: Well, I guess they're just too lazy to make two trips.

"I play the piano by ear."
"I listen the same way."

Dan: I challenge you to a battle of wits.
Stan: How brave of you to fight unarmed!

Mother: Sweet Charlotte, where's your little sister?
Charlotte: She's in the other room, Mother.
Mother: Well, go and see what she's doing and tell her to stop it.

Jeweller: That's a mighty sick-looking watch you have there.
Customer: *Yes, its hours are numbered.*

Husband (to Policeman): Officer, my wife has been throwing things at me ever since we've been married.
Policeman: *Then why didn't you complain before?*
Husband: This is the first time she's hit me.

Patrick: I once had to live on a can of beans for three days.
Michael: *My goodness, weren't you afraid of falling off?*

Frank: I hear they're going to have to fight the Battle of Bunker Hill over again.
Ernest: *Why?*
Frank: It wasn't fought on the level.

Slim: Did you know that I weighed only three pounds when I was born?
Stout: *You don't say! Did you live?*
Slim: Did I live? Boy, you ought to see me now!

Roy: I hear that fish is brain food.
Sylvester: *Yeah, I eat it all the time.*
Roy: Another theory disproved.

Customer: Is this a second-hand store?
Shop Assistant: *Yes.*
Customer: Good, I'd like to buy one for my watch.

"Say, Johnny, may I borrow your pen?"
    "Sure thing."
"Got a piece of writing paper I can use?"
    "Coming up."
"Going past the post box when you go out?"
    "Yeah."
"Wait a minute till I finish this letter, will you?"
    "All right."
"Want to lend me a stamp?"
    "Okay."
"Much obliged. Say, what's your girlfriend's address?"

Shaun: Ireland is the richest country in the world.
Mickey: Why do you say that?
Shaun: Because her capital has been Dublin for years.

Tillie: Do you like Kipling?
Millie: I don't know. I've never kippled.

Some people thirst after fame, some thirst after fortune, and some thirst after knowledge. But there's one thing everybody thirsts after — salted peanuts.

Uncle Zeke: Did you catch all those fish by yourself?
Smart Alex: Oh, no. I had a worm to help me.

Sid: Hey, Roy, if you don't stop playing that mouth
   organ you're gonna drive me crazy.
Roy: Too late, Sid. I stopped an hour ago.

Eve: Have you lived here all your life?
Steve: Not yet.

Ron: Are Ted's feet big?
*Don: I don't know. I've never seen him with his
   shoes off.*

"How's your insomnia?"
*"Worse. Now I can't even sleep when it's time to
   get up."*

Hal: Do you have any superstitions?
*Cal: No, I don't. I believe it's bad luck to be
   superstitious.*

"The police shot my dog."
"Was he mad?"
"Well, he wasn't too pleased about it."

Louie: Did you mark the spot where we caught all those fish?

Dewey: Yeah, I put a big X on the side of the boat.

Louie: But suppose we don't get the same boat next time?

Customer: I'd like to buy a mouse trap, and please hurry. I have to catch a train.

Shop Assistant: And what do you use for bait, sir?

Country Driver: We must be getting close to the city.

Wife: How can you tell?

Country Driver: We're running over more people.

"I just read where the Department of Commerce says that by 1991 there'll be 120 million cars in this country."

"I guess that if anybody wants to cross the road, they'd better do it now."

"Where's your heart?"

"Straight down my throat and first turn on the left."

Gert: I own 200 goldfish.

Myrt: Where do you keep them?

Gert: In the bathtub.

Myrt: What do you do when you want to take a bath?

Gert: I blindfold them.

"Fred Thompson called me a jackass."

"Don't stand for it."

"What'll I do?"

"Make him prove it."

Ed. I was born in Kentucky.

Ned: What part?

Ed: All of me.

Customer: Do you have anything for grey hair?

Barber: Only the greatest respect.

Ann: They say exercise kills germs.
Jan: *Yeah, but how do you get the little rascals to
exercise?*

"My Uncle Willie is worth in the area of twelve
million pounds."
"*That's my favourite area.*"

Hal: Grandma cured Grandpa of biting his nails.
Sal: *How did she do it?*
Hal: She hid his false teeth.

Jay: Did you see me when I came in that door?
Ray: *Yes.*
Jay: You never saw me before in your life, did you?
Ray: *No.*
Jay: Then how did you know it was me?

Tolliver: I've just been in a terrible fight.
Annabella: *Who won?*
Tolliver: I don't know. I left in the middle of it.

In the United States, the sister states are: Mary Land,
Ida ho, Louisa anna, and Minnie sota.

A young mountaineer built a new home for his bride,
but neglected to put any doors in it.
"*Where are the doors?*" inquired his bride.
"Doors?" replied the mountaineer. "What's the matter
— you going somewhere?"

Harvey and Herkimer were discussing the fact that so
many girls' names were the same as those of
cities.
"*Florence, Italy.*"
"Helena, Montana."
"*Elizabeth, New Jersey.*"
"Indianapolis, Indiana."
"*Just a minute, Harvey. Indianapolis isn't a girl's
name.*"
"Is that so? Do you know *everybody?*"

Gus: What's this kleptomania I've been reading about?
Is it catching?
Russ: No, it's taking.

Dick: Would you care to join me in a bowl of soup?
Nick: Do you suppose it's big enough for both of us?

"Where did you get that hat?"
"*ManHATtan.*"
"The coat?"
"*North DaCOATa.*"
"The vest?"
"*VEST Virginia.*"
"The collar?"
"*COLLARado.*"

Fay: Are ants intelligent?
May: Of course. How else could they figure out when you're having a picnic?

Little Alice was heartbroken when her pet canary
died, and to soften the blow, her father gave her a
cigar box for a coffin and assisted in burying the
canary in the back garden.
"*Daddy,*" whispered Little Alice after the funeral,
"*will my dear little birdie go to heaven?*"
"I expect so," replied her father. "Why?"
"*I was only thinking,*" murmured Little Alice, "*how
cross St. Peter will be when he opens the box and
discovers there are no cigars in it.*"

The little boy riding the bus had been sniffing for
several blocks.
*The lady sitting next to him said, "Little boy, don't
you have a handkerchief?"*
"Yes, ma'am," he replied, "but I never lend it to
strangers."

Gambling is an excellent method of getting nothing for
something.

Art: Where can I get hold of your sister?
Bart: I don't know. She's ticklish.

Mr. Dubbins arrived for work an hour late. His
 clothes were torn and tattered. He was banged
 and bruised, and he had one arm in a sling. His
 boss was purple with rage.
"It's ten o'clock," screamed the boss. "You were
 supposed to be here at nine. What happened?"
"I'm sorry," explained Mr. Dubbins, "I fell out of a
 ten-storey window."
"This took you a whole hour?"

Ray: May I see you pretty soon?
Kay: Don't you think I'm pretty, now?

"My name is Charles S. Munchinson."
"What does the S stand for?"
"Nothing. My father dropped a noodle on my birth
 certificate."

Gloria: If you want a date with me, you'll have to wait
 a million years.
Jack: But I'm the only boy left in town.
Gloria: My, how time flies!

Alfred was puzzled about a social problem and
 consulted his friend Mortimer.
"I have walked Evelyn home from school every day for
 a week. I carried her books for her. I bought her
 two pineapple sundaes. Now, do you think I ought
 to kiss her?"
"No," answered Mortimer, "I think you've done
 enough for her already."

"The baby swallowed a whole bottle of ink."
"Incredible!"
"No, indelible."

Ernie: This liniment makes my arm smart.
Bernie: Why not rub some on your head?

Usher: How far down do you wish to sit?
Sweet Little Old Lady: All the way. I'm very tired.

14

Athlete: Can you stand on your head?
Second Athlete: Of course not, it's too high.

Father: Why is Egbert sticking out his tongue?
Mother: I guess the doctor forgot to tell him to put
   it back in.

A woman was standing in front of the hippopotamus'
   cage at the zoo. She asked the attendant, "Is your
   hippo a male or female?"
"That madam," replied the attendant, "is a question
   that should only interest another hippopotamus."

Rubbing hair restorer into your scalp very vigorously
will give you hairy fingertips.

Hy: Were you lucky at the horse races yesterday?
Sy: Was I ever! I found a 50 pence on the ground
   after the last race, so I didn't have to walk home.

Willis: Did you knit that sweater all by yourself?
Phyllis: Yes, all except the hole you put your head
   through. That was already there when I started.

Customer: How much are your twenty pound shoes?
Shop Assistant: Ten pounds a foot.

Husband: The bank just returned this cheque you
   wrote!
Wife: Oh, wonderful! Now I can use it again to buy
   something else.

A hunter was bragging about his marksmanship.
"See that polar bear rug on the floor? That bear
   was only five feet away when I shot him. It was a
   case of me or him!"
"Well," yawned his weary listener, "the bear certainly
   makes a better rug."

Mr. Binner, on his way to work, passed a window where he saw a lady hitting a boy over the head with a loaf of bread. Mr. Binner decided it was none of his business, so he continued on his way. This went on every day for five months. Each morning Mr. Binner would pass the window and see the lady hitting the boy over the head with a loaf of bread.

Then, one morning, he looked in the window and saw the lady hitting the boy over the head with a chocolate cake. Astounded, Mr. Binner stuck his head in the window and asked the lady why she was hitting the boy over the head with a chocolate cake, instead of a loaf of bread.

"Oh," said the lady, "today's his birthday."

For an important opening night, a couple received a pair of theatre tickets, anonymously sent.

They phoned all their friends to find out who'd sent the tickets, but to no avail. Nobody knew who sent them. They racked their brains saying, "From whom? From whom?"

Opening night, they attended the theatre. It was an excellent performance, but they couldn't enjoy it properly, for worrying about where the tickets came from.

When they got home from the show, they found their apartment ransacked. Every single thing of any value had been stolen, and on the table was a note reading, *"Now you know from whom!"*

Fred and Ned were crossing a field when a bull came charging down upon them. Fred quickly climbed a nearby tree, and Ned dived down into a hole. The bull leaped over the hole, and Ned jumped out. The bull turned, saw Ned, and charged at him again. This happened several times.

Finally, Fred yelled down at Ned, *"If you don't stay down in the hole, the bull will never stop charging you, and we'll never get home."*

The bull charged, and Ned dived into the hole again. The next time he jumped out, he yelled at Fred, *"I can't stay down in the hole. There's a bear in there!"*

Taxi Driver (to Passenger): I forgot to turn on the meter and I don't know how much to charge you.
Passenger: That's okay. I forgot to bring money, so I can't pay you anyway.

Lady (to Shop Assistant): I'd like to buy a sweater for my dog.
Shop Assistant: What size?
Lady: I have no idea.
Shop Assistant: Well, why don't you bring in the dog and try one on?
Lady: Oh, I can't do that. I want it to be a surprise!

A woman at the movies turned and said to the man behind her, "If my hat prevents your seeing the picture, I'll be happy to remove it."

"Please don't bother," replied the man. "Your hat is much funnier than the picture."

"Little Jimmy," said his mother, "did you fall down with your good trousers on?"

"Yes, Mother," replied Jimmy. "There wasn't time to take them off."

Martha: Did you make the debating team?

Arthur: N-n-n-n-no, they s-s-s-s-said I wasn't t-t-t-t-tall enough.

A little girl from the South was seeing snow for the first time. "Oh mummy," she cried excitedly, "what is it?"

"That's snow, dear," answered her mother. "What did you think it was?"

"It looks like iced rain!"

Mollie: Why are you running?

Ollie: To stop a fight.

Mollie: Who's fighting?

Ollie: Me and another fellow.

RIDDLE DE DEE

What do you put on only when it's wet?
> *A coat of paint.*

What has sixteen legs?
> *Four rabbits.*

What is at the end of everything?
> *The letter g.*

What colours would you paint the sun and the wind?
> *The sun rose and the wind blue.*

What pets make exciting music?
> *Trum-pets.*

What does the envelope say when you lick it?
> *It just shuts up and says nothing.*

Why is an island like the letter t?
> *Both are in the middle of water.*

How do you get down from an elephant?
> *You don't get down from an elephant. You get down from a duck.*

What's the difference between a thief and a church bell?

One steals from the people. The other peals from the steeple.

What has eyes but can't see?
A potato.

What has legs, but can't walk?
A bed.

What has three feet, but no toes?
A yardstick.

What has hands and a face, but can't touch or smile?
A clock.

What works only when it's fired?
A rocket.

What has teeth, but no mouth?
A comb.

What has wings, but can't fly?
A mansion.

What has leaves, but is not a plant?
A table.

What looks empty when full?
A balloon.

What has a mouth, but no teeth?
A river.

What has ears, but can't hear?
Corn.

What has arms, but no hands?
A chair.

When fish swim in schools, who helps out the teacher?
The Herring aid.

Why do chickens never get rich?
Because they work for chicken feed.

What do vultures always have for dinner?
Leftovers.

What do patriotic American monkeys wave on Flag day?
Star spangled bananas.

Why is an empty purse always the same?
Because there's never any change in it.

How many hot dogs can you eat on an empty stomach?
Only one, because after that your stomach is no longer empty.

Why is it bad to write a letter on an empty stomach?
Because it's much better to write on paper.

Who can marry many a wife and still remain single all of his life?
A minister.

What do you take off last before getting into bed?
Your feet off the floor.

What is everyone in the world doing at the same time?
Growing older.

Why isn't your nose twelve inches long?
Because then it would be a foot.

When are your eyes not eyes?
When the wind makes them water.

What time is it when you see an elephant sitting on your fence?
Time to buy a new fence.

If you threw a green shoe into the Red Sea, what would it become?
Wet.

Why is paper money more valuable than coins?
When you put it in your pocket you double it.
When you take it out it's in creases.

What's the difference between a jeweller and a jailer?
One sells watches, while the other watches cells.

What goes 99-clump, 99-clump, 99-clump?
A centipede with a wooden leg.

Which burns longer — the candles on a girl's birthday cake, or the candles on a boy's birthday cake?
Neither. They both burn shorter.

Why is a baseball game like a pancake?
Because they both depend on the batter.

What's the difference between here and there?
The letter t.

What do you serve, but never eat?
A tennis ball.

In what month do people talk the least?
February — because it's the shortest.

Why is a rabbit's nose always shiny?
Because she has her powder puff on the wrong end.

What has a foot at each end and a foot in the middle?
A yardstick.

Where did Noah keep his bees?
In the Ark hives.

What's white when it's dirty?
A blackboard.

What's the difference between a locomotive engineer
and a school teacher?
One minds the train, and the other trains the mind.

Why do they put mirrors on chewing-gum machines?
So you can see what you look like when the chewing gum doesn't come out.

What goes, "Oom, oom, oom."?
A cow walking backwards.

How many sides has a box?
Two. The inside and the outside.

What do hippopotamuses have that no other animals have?
Baby hippopotamuses.

What bird can be heard at meals?
A swallow.

What's the best way to drive a baby buggy?
Tickle its little feet.

How many big men were born in Massachusetts?
None. Only babies were born there.

When is it socially correct to serve milk in a saucer?
When you're feeding the cat.

What has one horn, runs up and down the street, and gives milk?
A milk truck.

How do you keep milk from turning sour?
Leave it inside the cow.

Which is faster — hot or cold?
Hot's faster. You can catch a cold.

What word is always pronounced wrong?
Wrong.

What's the longest word in the dictionary?
Smiles. There's a mile between the first and last letter.

If you see ten little tomatoes all in a row, which one is the cowboy?
None. They're all redskins.

Why did Robin Hood only rob the rich?
Because the poor had no money.

Why did the wheel get a liberal education?
Because it wanted to be well rounded.

What's grey, has very large ears, four legs and a trunk?
A mouse taking a sea voyage.

What's the difference between a hill and a pill?
One is hard to get up and the other is hard to get down.

Name two things you can never eat before breakfast.
Lunch and dinner.

A doctor, a lawyer, and a chicken inspector are all walking down the street together. Which one wears the largest hat?
The one with the largest head.

What's the difference between a glamorous movie star and a small mouse?
One charms hes and the other harms cheese.

Why does Uncle Sam wear red, white and blue braces?
To hold up his trousers.

What's the difference between a man going up the stairs and a man looking up the stairs?

One steps up the stairs and the other stares up the steps.

Why is it easier to wash a mirror than a window?

Because a window has two sides.

What has four wheels, two horns, gives milk, and eats grass?

A cow on a skateboard.

What did the surgeon say to the patient?

"Suture self."

What is pear shaped, yellowish-red, and costs six million dollars?

The Bionic Mango.

Why can't you trust comedians?

Because they're always pulling some kind of funny business.

When Hawaiians play basketball, what do they use for nets?

Hoola hoops.

What game do mother hens play with their babies?

Peck-a-boo.

Why do birds fly south for the winter?

Because they can't afford to take the train.

What did Cinderella Fish wear to the ball?

Glass flippers.

Where do fish keep their life savings?
In a river bank.

Why did Sir Lancelot take a torch into his bedroom?
Because he was afraid to sleep without a knight light on.

Why do buffaloes always travel in herds?
Because they're afraid of getting mugged by elephants.

Who fights crime, eats bread crumbs, and has a secret identity?
Bat Mouse and Robin, the bird wonder.

Why did the girl ask her boyfriend to write her a love letter in the sand?
Because she needed something to tide her over.

What is the favourite card game of pigs?
Draw porker.

Which pig fought in the American Revolution and later became the first President?
George Washingham.

What runs around the garden, keeps strangers away from your house, and has five hundred teeth?
A picket fence.

When were the Dark Ages?
During the days of the knights.

Who was the famous chicken who rode with the Rough Riders and later became President?
Teddy Roostervelt.

What's yellow, swims in the ocean, and swallows ships?
Moby Banana.

Why did the bus driver go broke?
Because he drove all of his customers away.

What did the stereo say to the record?
"Hi, baby. How about going for a spin?"

If a man married a princess, what would he be?
Her husband.

What's the difference between an excited skunk and a calm skunk?
A twenty-pound laundry bill.

How does a cowboy drive a herd of steer?
He turns their steering wheels.

If a skin diver loses his compass, how can he tell which way to go?
He can look at the north starfish.

What does Santa Claus say when he works in the garden?
"Hoe-Hoe-Hoe!"

What weighs three tons, flies, and pulls Santa's sleigh?
Rudolph the Red-Nosed Rhinoceros.

Who invented the first aeroplane that didn't fly?
Orville and Wilbur Wrong.

What did the waterfall say to the water fountain?
"You're nothing but a little squirt."

Why do kettles whistle?
Because they never learned to sing.

Which fruit is always sad?
Blueberries.

Where can you always find a helping hand?
At the end of your arm.

What kind of paper do you use to make a kite?
Fly paper, of course.

What do you get when a herd of elephants stampede
through a field of corn and beans?
Succotash.

What's the difference between a tiny elephant and a
gigantic mouse?
About 3,000 pounds.

What happens to two frogs who try to catch the same
insect at the same time?
They end up tongue-tied.

Why did the father call his son Bulb?
Because the boy was the light of his life.

What would you call a cow that sits on the grass?
Four hundred pounds of ground beef.

What did the optician say to his glasses?
"Stop making spectacles of yourselves."

What time is it when an elephant climbs into your bed?
Time to get a new bed.

Why is a tennis court so noisy?
Because every player on it raises a racket.

What is the fastest way to go to the hospital?
Pick a fight with an elephant.

What does a polite mouse always say?
"Cheese and thank you."

Why did the corn go to the doctor's office?
Because it had an earache.

What's the best way to come face to face with a timid mouse?
Lie down in front of a mouse hole and cover your nose with cheese spread.

What's the best way to get a rhino's attention?
Honk his horn.

What has wings, smokes, and walks on ceilings?
A fire-breathing dragonfly.

What do termites eat for dessert?
Toothpicks.

If Mounties always get their man, what do postmen always get?

Their mail.

What did the rabbit give his girlfriend when he proposed to her?

A 24-carrot ring.

What happens when a flock of geese land in a volcano?

They cook their own gooses.

What game do rabbits always love to play?

Hopscotch.

What did the girl say to the boy she wanted to marry?

"Why don't you give me a ring sometime?"

Why do hummingbirds hum?

Because they can't remember the words.

How can you tell if an elephant is a mugger?

He'll be wearing a balaclava and hiding in a dark alley.

Why are giraffes good friends to have?

Because they're willing to stick their necks out.

Why do elephants have trunks?

Because they'd look silly wearing suitcases on their noses.

Why do baby birds never smile?

Would you smile if your mother fed you worms for dinner every night?

What did Hamlet name his little boy?
Piglet.

Where do sharks do their shopping?
At fish markets.

What do you call the autobiography cf a shark?
A fish story.

What is the safest way to pick an apple off the top of a fifty-foot-tall tree?
Chop down the tree, then pick the apple.

What's purple, lives in the jungle, and is always on a vine?
Tarzan the Grape Man.

What did the boy say when the Statue of Liberty sneezed?
"God Bless, America!"

What kind of vegetables do llamas like to eat?
Llama lima beans.

Why is a hen sitting on a fence like a penny?
Because she has a head on one side and a tail on the other.

What do cannibals eat for dessert?
Bawanna splits.

Can lightbulbs see?
Only if they have electric eyes.

Who has magical powers, a big nose, and lives in an Emerald City?
The Wizard of Schnoz.

What is the easiest thing for a trapper to catch in a tropical rain forest?
A cold.

Why didn't the travelling elephant tip the bellboy when he checked into the hotel?
Because the bellboy didn't carry the elephant's trunk to his room.

What is faster than a speeding bullet, bends steel, and eats tall buildings in a single bite?
Super Termite

Why do salmon swim upstream to spawn?
Because walking along the riverbank hurts their tails.

What's grey, has two wheels, and weighs four tons?
An elephant on a motorcycle.

How does an elephant get out of a Volkswagen?
The same way he got in.

What's the best way to tell an elephant with a short temper that he's fired?
You call him long distance.

Why did the bald man buy a rabbit farm?
Because he wanted to grow some hares.

Why did the little dog almost itch to death?
Because he was so gentle that he wouldn't hurt a flea.

What happens when the human body is completely submerged in water?
The telephone rings.

How can you make trousers last?
Make the coat and vest first.

Why is a bell the most obedient thing in the world?
Because it never speaks till it is tolled.

What do you have when you collect 100 female hogs and 100 male deer?
Two hundred sows and bucks.

What's the difference between a prize fighter and a person with a bad cold?
One knows his blows, and the other blows his nose.

Why did the moth eat a hole in the rug?
Because it wanted to see the floor show.

What does a worm do in a cornfield?
It goes in one ear and out the other.

How can you make a slow horse fast?
Stop feeding him.

On which side does an eagle have the most feathers?
The outside.

What is it that is always behind the time?
The back of a clock.

If ten birds were sitting on a branch and you shot one, how many would be left?

None. They would all fly away.

If twelve make a dozen, how many make a million?

Very few.

What weighs three tons, has tusks, and loves pepperoni pizza?

An Italian circus elephant.

What did one wig say to the other?

"I love you so much I'd even curl up and dye for you."

How do you catch an elephant?

You buy a fishing pole and put a peanut on the hook.

Where do jellyfish get their jelly?

From ocean currents.

How can you tell when a tree is really frightened?

It'll be petrified.

Why is a school playground larger at breaktime?

Because there are more feet in it.

Who caught flies with his tongue and was the first treasurer of the United States?

Salamander Hamilton.

What does the sneezing champion of the Olympics win?

A Cold Medal.

What follows a dog wherever he goes?
His tail.

Why are spiders good baseball players?
Because they know how to catch flies.

What has spots, weighs four tons, and loves peanuts?
An elephant with the measles.

What is big, likes peanuts, and has a trunk?
An oak tree with a squirrel in it.

What is green and pecks on trees?
Woody Wood Pickle.

What do you call a hot-dog who always speaks his mind?
A frank-furter.

Why do tigers have stripes?
Because they'd look funny in polka dots.

What has two feet, a high-powered rifle, and spots before its eyes?
A hunter shooting at a leopard.

What did the eloping groom say to his bride when the ladder broke?
"We cantaloupe."

What parts of Berlin are in France?
The letters e, r, and n.

How do you quiet down a noisy dog?
You put him in a "No Barking" zone.

Where do moles go to get married?
To the tunnel of love.

What eats peanuts, weighs four tons, and goes, "Sniffle Sniffle, Ah-Choo!"?
An elephant with a bad cold.

What did the topsoil say to the thunderstorm?
"If this keeps up, my name will be mud!"

How can you tell if a cat burglar has been in your house?
Your cat will be missing!

What do you call a duck physician?
A quack doctor.

What do you call a slim parrot?
Polly-unsaturated.

What do you call a cabbage that gossips?
A gabbage.

How do you tell how old a telephone is?
You count its rings.

How did the nervous carpenter break his teeth?
He bit his nails.

Where do bunny rabbits like to spend their vacations?
On Easter Island.

What lives in the ocean, is grouchy, and hates neighbours?
A hermit crab.

What do you call it when the members of an orchestra go on social security.
Band-aid.

What's black and white, white and black, and green?
Two skunks fighting over a pickle.

What is brown, likes peanuts, and is covered with oil?
A french fried elephant.

Why is a kiss like gossip?
Because it goes from mouth to mouth.

KNOCKKNOCKS

Who's there?
Arthur.
Arthur Who?
Arthur mometer is broken.

Who's there?
Choo-choo train.
Choo-choo train who?
Choo-choo trained the lion, but he had trouble getting the tiger to cooperate.

Who's there?
Isabel.
Isabel who?
Isabel out of order?

Who's there?
Senior.
Senior who?
Senior uncle lately?

Who's there?
Ferry.
Ferry who?
Ferry tales can come true.

Who's there?
Heel.
Heel who?
Heel be right back.

Who's there?
Osborn.
Osborn who?
Osborn in the state of Georgia.

Who's there?
Elder.
Elder who?
Elder in my arms all evening.

Who's there?
Peeper.
Peeper who?
Peeper and salt, that's who.

Who's there?
Canopy.
Canopy who?
Canopy you by check?

Who's there?
Pecan.
Pecan who?
Pecan somebody your own size.

Who's there?
Della.
Della who?
Della-Catessan.

Who's there?
Tom.
Tom who?
Tom orrow is another day.

Who's there?
Fire engine.
Fire engine who?
Fire engine one and prepare for blast-off.

38

Who's there?
Sherwood.
Sherwood who?
Sherwood like for you to let me in.

Who's there?
Thistle.
Thistle who?
Thistle make you whistle.

Who's there?
Pressure.
Pressure who?
Pressure shirt?

Who's there?
Mandy.
Mandy who?
Mandy lifeboats.

Who's there?
Doctor.
Doctor who?
Doctor a day's pay for not coming to work.

Who's there.
Hyena.
Hyena who?
Hyena tree sat the owl.

Who's there?
Tuba.
Tuba who?
Tuba toothpaste.

Who's there?
Boo-hoo.
Boo-hoo who?
Boo-hoo-hoo.
Boo-hoo-hoo who?
Boo-hoo-hoo-hoo.
Boo-hoo-hoo-hoo who?
Boo-hoo-hoo-hoo-hoo.
Boo-hoo-hoo-hoo-hoo who?
Stop it? Your breaking my heart!

Who's there?
Vera.
Vera Who?
Vera interesting.

Who's there?
Nobody.
Thank goodness!

Who's there?
Hence.
Hence who?
Hence lay eggs.

Who's there?
Oliver.
Oliver who?
Oliver troubles will soon be over.

Who's there?
You.
You who?
Yoo hoo, yourself.

Who's there
Orange Juice.
Orange Juice who?
Orange juice sorry you made me cry?

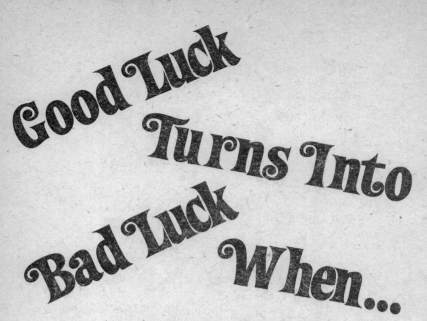

Good Luck Turns Into Bad Luck When...

... a rhino is chasing you and you find a nearby tree to climb ... only to find an ape in it.

... a neighbourhood layabout finally pays back the twenty pounds he owes you ... and the money turns out to be counterfeit.

... cockroaches evacuate your house ... only because termites are moving in.

... you call the credit card company to tell them they made a mistake on your bill ... and they agree with you only because they didn't charge you enough.

... you break a leg in front of a doctor's office ... and the doctor turns out to be an optician.

... lightning misses you and strikes a nearby tree ... and the tree falls on you.

... the handsomest boy in school calls you up ... and then apologises because he dialled the wrong number.

... you pick up a looseball and run ninety yards for a try ... only to find out you ran the wrong way.

... it snows so much that you don't have to go to school ... and you end up spending the whole day shovelling the driveway and pavement.

... you get an "A" on a surprise quiz in school ... and the teacher decides not to count the grade.

... you hit a six to win the game ... and the ball goes through a neighbour's front window.

FUNNY PUPPETS

Karate Expert Puppet: *You put your hand into it, and it breaks your wrist.*

Politician Puppet: *You put your hand into it, and it smiles and shakes your other hand.*

Debt Collector Puppet: *You put your hand into it, and it holds out its other hand.*

Visiting Aunt Puppet: *You put your hand into it, and it gives you a sloppy kiss on the forehead.*

Little Brat Puppet: *You put your hand into it, and it sticks its tongue out at you.*

Nurse Puppet: *You put your hand into it, and it takes your pulse.*

Film Star Puppet: *You put your hand into it, and it signs its autograph on your arm.*

Pickpocket Puppet: *You put your hand into it, and it puts its hand into your pocket.*

Motorcycle Cop Puppet: *You put your hand into it, and it writes out a speeding ticket.*

Dieting Puppet: *You put your hand into it, and it raids the refrigerator.*

Mean School Teacher Puppet: *You put your hand into it, and it cracks you across the knuckles with a tiny ruler.*

DIZZY DAFFYNITIONS

Alarm Clock: *A mechanical device to wake up people who don't have small children.*

Ash Tray: *Something to put ash in if a room doesn't have a floor.*

Authorship: *A large seagoing vessel belonging to a writer.*

Autobiography: *The life story of an automobile.*

Billow: *What a man with a bad cold sleeps with his head on.*

Bore: *One who opens his mouth and puts his feats in.*

Boss: *A man who is at the office early on the days when you're late.*

Boycott: *A bed for a small male child.*

Bread: *Raw toast.*

Cartoon: *A song sung in an automobile.*

Caterpillar: *An upholstered worm.*

Chilli: *An internal hot-foot.*

Circle: *A round straight line with a hole in the middle.*

College: *A mental institution.*

Comedian: *A person with a good memory who hopes other people haven't.*

Confidence: *The feeling you have before you know better.*

Cowardice: *Yellow, frozen water.*

Cuisine: *Any food that you can't pronounce.*

Denial: *A river in Egypt.*

Dieting: *The triumph of mind over platter.*

Divine: *What da grapes grow on.*

Dog Show: *Oodles of poodles.*

Duck: *A bird that looks as if it has been riding a horse all day.*

Egotist: *Someone who is always me-deep in conversation.*

Eiffel Tower: *A French mecanno set that made good.*

Eye Dropper: *A very, very careless person.*

Flashlight: *A case in which to carry dead batteries.*

Flood: *A river too big for its bridges.*

Forger: *A person who is always ready to write a wrong.*

Gossip: *Rumourtism.*

Grand Canyon: *Hole of Fame.*

Grudge: *A place to keep an car.*

Harp: *A nude piano.*

Hug: *Energy that has gone to waist.*

Ideal: *My turn to shuffle.*

Infant Prodigy: *A small child with highly imaginative parents.*

Laugh: *A smile that burst.*

Lawsuit: *A policeman's uniform.*

Lecture: *Something that makes you feel numb at one end and dumb at the other.*

Lost-and-Found Department: *A place where people take things they've found and have no use for.*

Middle Ages: *The "Knight" time.*

Mischief: *The chief's daughter.*

Missing: *To sing incorrectly.*

Mosquito: *A small insect designed by nature to make us think better of flies.*

Mountain Climber: *Someone who wants to take a peak.*

Net Income: *The money a fisherman earns.*

Paradox: *Two medical doctors.*

Parasols: *Two men named Sol.*

Pessimist: *Someone who's never happy unless he's miserable.*

Poise: *The ability to continue talking while the other fellow picks up the bill.*

Police Helicopter: *The whirlybird that catches the worm.*

Professor: *Someone who goes to college and never gets out.*

Raisin: *A worried grape.*

Scotland Yard: *Three feet — the same as anywhere else.*

Skeleton: *Bones with people scraped off.*

Snoring: *Sheet music.*

Spanking: *Stern punishment.*

Steam: *Water gone crazy with the heat.*

Sweater: *A garment worn by a small child when his mother feels chilly.*

Synonym: *The word you use in place of the one you can't spell.*

Taxpayers: *People who don't have to take a civil service test to work for the government.*

Tricycle: *A tot rod.*

Unabridged: *A river you have to wade across.*

Window Shopper: *A store gazer.*

World: *A big ball that revolves on its taxes.*

Last year the dynamiters' union held a New Year's Eve party and it was a real blast.

"My Aunt Lily loves to go swimming."
"*Maybe she's a water lily.*"

Judy: What's the best thing to do if you're going to be beheaded?
Tina: Stay calm and try not to lose your head.

I know an Indian rubber man who's a compulsive liar. He's always stretching the truth.

"I'm happy because I just filled up my car with petrol."
"*Now that's what I call being tankful.*"

Lance: Did you hear that all of the members of King Arthur's Round Table have insomnia?
Merlin: Wow! That's what I call having a lot of sleepless knights.

Jill: Minks are very charitable animals.
Lill: How do you know that?
Jill: When minks see rich people who need new coats, they give them the shirts right off their backs.

Dom: Did you hear about the accident at the glue factory? A vat of glue spilled all over the floor.
Tom: Boy! I'll bet that was a sticky situation.

"Why aren't you the president of the mortgage department anymore?"
"Well to tell the truth, I lost interest."

Bill: Did you hear about the cross-eyed dog who chased a cat until it climbed out of reach?
Will: No. What happened?
Bill: The dog ended up barking up the wrong tree.

Joe: Have you ever met the Invisible Man?
Moe: No, but I hear he's out of sight!

"Would you ever want to drive a taxi-cab for a living?"
"No I just couldn't hack the long hours."

A policeman who moonlights in a rock band as a drummer pounds a beat both night and day.

"How did you like the story about the Abominable Snowman?"
"It left me cold."

Jerry: It's been a long day.
Perry: It sure has. I've been up since the crack of yawn.

Judy: Your trousers look sad today.
Rudy: What do you mean?
Judy: Sort of depressed.

What is the secret of success?
    "Push," said the doorbell.
    "Never be lead," said the pencil.
    "Take panes," said the window.
    "Always keep cool," said the ice.
    "Never lose your head," said the drum.
    "Make light of everything," said the fire.
    "Do a driving business," said the hammer.
    "Aspire to 'grater' things," said the nutmeg.
    "Be sharp in all your dealings," said the knife.
    "Find a good thing and stick to it," said the glue.

Beggar: Can you help a poor man? I need bread.

Professor: *Explain that a little better. Do you need bread or knead bread? I mean are you a beggar that loafs or a loafer that begs?*

Customer: See here, photographer, this picture you took of me is awful. Do you call it a good likeness?

Photographer: *The answer, sir, is in the negative.*

Hunter: Holy cow! Here comes a bunch of cannibals!

Guide: *Sh! Don't get yourself in a stew.*

"I spent last year in a city in Switzerland."

"*Berne?*"

"No, I darn near froze."

Sue: Did you ever see the Catskill Mountains?

Clu: *No, but I've seen cats kill mice.*

The magician's wife knew he was up to his old tricks because she found a hare on his shoulder.

Jane: I can't marry you, Joe — you're penniless.

Joe: *That's nothing — the Czar of Russia was Nicholas.*

Jon: Why did you become a printer?

Ron: *I guess I'm just the right type.*

"My name is St. Peter. How did you get here to heaven?"

"*Flu!*"

Bennie: What's the witching hour?

Jennie: *It's when you come home late from school and your mother says, "Which story is it this time?"*

"Do you have much fish in your basket?"
"Yes, a good eel."

Reporter: There's been a terrible murder in the
rooming-house. A paper-hanger hung a border.
Editor: It must've been a put-up job.

He: Darling, here's a diamond engagement ring for you.
*She: Thanks, honey, but the diamond has a flaw in
it.*
He: You shouldn't notice that. You're in love and love
is blind.
She: Right, but not stone blind.

"It's raining cats and dogs outside."
"I know, I just stepped into a poodle."

Len: I'm a pauper.
Ben: Congratulations. Boy or Girl?

Are the Michiganders any relation to the Portuguese?

At a baseball game, Mary was struck on the head, and
a bawl came out of her mouth.

Joanie: Imagine! A man diving from a height of 60 feet
into a pail of water!
Tony: So what? It's only a drop in the bucket.

Wife: I heard that our neighbour beats his wife up
every morning.
Husband: No kidding!
Wife: Yep — he gets up at eight, and she gets up at
nine.

"My twins have just fallen down the well! What shall
   I do?"
*"Go down to the library and ask for that book: How To
   Bring Up Children."*

Clem: I saw a big rat in my cooker and when I went for
   my revolver, he ran out.
Clyde: Did you shoot him?
Clem: No, he was out of my range.

Waiter: With that bushy moustache of yours, don't you
   find it hard to eat soup?
Customer: Sure, it's quite a strain.

Customer: Chemist, give me some consecrated lye.
Chemist: You mean concentrated lye, don't you, sir?
Customer: It does nutmeg any difference. That's what I
   camphor. What does it sulfur?
Chemist: Fifteen pence.

"If a man smashed a clock, could he be accused of
   killing time?"
"Not if he could prove that the clock struck first."

Millie: Willie, what's a Greek urn?
Willie: Oh, about 40 drachmas a week.

Diner: Waiter, this coffee is sheer mud.
Waiter: Sorry, sir, but it was only ground this morning.

"Dr Jekyll, tell me more about your other self."
"Beat it — you're getting under my Hyde."

Guide: Going to hunt lions this season, as usual?
Hunter: No. I am going to look for gnu game.

He made a fortune in crooked dough — he's a pretzel-maker.

"Tough luck!" said the egg in the monastery. "Out of the frying pan into the friar."

Jill: You've been drinking beer. I can smell it on your breath.
Will: *No, I've been eating frogs' legs. What you smell is the hops.*

Parting advice — look in the mirror while using your comb.

"Why do you call this awful place the Fiddle Hotel?"
"*Because it's such a vile inn.*"

Cutomer: Have you anything snappy in rubber bands.
Shopkeeper: *No, but we have something catchy in fly-paper.*

Jill: I'll stick to you like glue.
Will: *The feeling is mucilage.*

"I've come to see General Parker."
"*I'm sorry, but the general is sick today.*"
"What made him sick?"
"*Oh, things in general.*"

He: My name's Dunlop. Can you make a pun on it?
She: *Sure — lop off the last syllable and it's Dun.*

Don: On the ocean, why do they use knots instead of miles?
Ron: *Because they've got to have the ocean tide.*

"Look here comes a Turk. I can't remember his name, but his fez is familiar."

"If you want your parrot to talk you should begin by teaching it short words."
"Really? I thought it would be quicker to use polly-syllables."

Minister: Do you take this woman for butter or for wurst.
Groom: Oh, liver alone. I never sausage nerve.

"Who was the smallest man in history?"
"The Roman soldier who went to sleep on his watch."

Artie: Did you hear about the guy who ate 79 pancakes?
Marty: Oh, how waffle!

Always remember — no matter how bad prose may be, it might be verse.

Better to have loved a short girl than never to have loved a tall.

Knott and Shott fought a duel with pistols. Knott was shot and Shott was not. It was better to be Shott than Knott.

Song of the hive: *"Bee it ever so humble, there's no place like comb."*

"Honey why can't we take a trip on a boat?"
"Because beggars can't be cruisers, dear."

Homer: How did the play they put on in the jail turn out?
Gomer: Great — it was a cell out.

The printer who set in type £10,000 to read £1,000 might have prevented his mistake by a little fourth-aught.

... a small child who won't make up his mind?
A maybe baby.

... a layabout who's been caught in the rain?
A damp tramp.

... a bird who lives around cows?
A dairy canary.

... a stupid ruler?
A ding-a-ling king.

... a naked rabbit?
A bare hare.

... a bloody yarn?
A gory story.

... a giant fish at half price?
A whale sale.

... breakfast food for spirits?
Ghosties Toasties.

... a ghost on crutches?
A hobblin' goblin.

... sweets dropped on the beach?
Sandy candy.

... a tired tent?
A sleepy teepee.

... strange whiskers?
A weird beard.

... a wet seal?
A damp stamp.

... an insane flower?
a crazy daisy.

... a fake horse?
A phony pony.

... a slippery razor?
A slick bic.

... a fortunate water-bird?
A lucky duckie.

... arithmetic trails
Maths paths.

... a rodent who lives indoors?
A house mouse.

... a cruel ruler?
A mean queen.

... an insect's car?
A roach coach.

... a baby cow's answer to a joke?
A calf laugh.

... the notes a rabbit uses to pay his debts?
Bunny money.

... a nasty bug that eats up the poor farmer's cotton?
An evil weevil.

... a witch's suitcase?
A hag bag.

... a conversation between two large birds?
Stork talk.

... a shortage of head coverings?
A cap gap.

... a 747 puppy?
A jet pet.

FOR BETTER OR VERSE

Hickory, dickory, dock,
Two mice ran up the clock,
The clock struck one,
But the other one got away.

I eat my peas with honey,
I've done it all my life;
It may seem kinda funny,
But they don't roll off my knife.

'Twixt optimist and pessimist,
The difference is droll:
The optimist sees the doughnut,
The pessimist sees the hole.

I sneezed a sneeze into the air,
It fell to the earth I know not where;
Hard and cold were the looks of those
In whose vicinity I snooze.

"I guess it must be time to go,"
At last remarked the bore;
"A wonderful guess," she answered,
"Why didn't you guess before?"

At railroad crossings,
Here's how to figure:
In case of a tie,
The train is bigger.

"I love the ground you walk on."
This was the tale he told;
For they lived up in the Klondike,
And the ground was full of gold.

Said little Jimmy to the owl:
"I've heard you're wonderous wise
And so I'd like to question you,
Now, please don't tell me lies;
I've heard it said, yet do not know,
In fact it may be bosh,
Then tell me, is it lots of dirt
That makes Seattle, Wash?"

"This is a time of mounting debts,
As you must surely know;
This secret then impart to me,
How much does Cleveland, O?"

"In ages, too, you must be learned
More so than many men;
So tell me in a whisper, please,
When was Miss Nashville, Tenn?"

"Some voices are so strong and full
And some so still and small
That I have wondered often times —
How loud can Denver, Col?"

The owl scratched his feathered pate;
"I'm sorry, little man,
Ask someone else, I cannot tell —
Perhaps Topeka, Kan."

I remember, I remember
Ere my childhood flitted by,
It was cold then in December
And was warmer in July.
In the winter there were freezings,
In the summer there were thaws;
But the weather isn't now at all
Like what it used to was.

I said, "This horse, sir, will you
    shoe?"
And soon the horse was shod.
I said, "This deed, sir, will you do?"
And soon the deed was dod!
I said, "This stick, sir, will you
    break?"
At once the stick he broke.
I said, "This coat, sir, will you
    make?"
And soon the coat he moke.

My name is Ebenezer;
'Tis a name I much despise,
And oh how quick I'll drop it
When rich Uncle Ebbie dies.

A June bug married an angle worm.
An accident cut her in two,
They charged the bug with bigamy;
Now what could the poor thing do?

'Twas ever thus, from childhood's
    hour,
That chilling fate has on me fell.
There always comes a soaking
    shower
When I ain't got no umberell.

The curfew tolls the knell of parting
    day,
A line of cars winds slowly o'er the
    lea.
A pedestrian plods his absent-
    minded way
And leaves the world quite
    unexpectedly.

He who stops
To look each way
Will live to drive
Another day.
But he who crashes
Through the red
May wake up once
And find he's dead.

How sweet to waken in the morn,
When sunbeams first begin to creep
Across the lea — and then to lie
Right back again and go to sleep.

Beneath this grassy mound now
rests
One Edgar Oscar Earl,
Who to another hunter looked
Exactly like a squirrel.

If all the land were apple pie,
And all the seas were ink;
And all the trees were bread and
cheese,
What would we do for drink?

The night was growing old
As he trudged through snow and
sleet;
His nose was long and cold,
And his shoes were full of feet.

I dreamed a dream next Tuesday
week
Beneath the apple trees;
I thought my eyes
Were big pork pies
And my nose was Cheddar cheese.
The clock struck twenty minutes to
six
When a frog sat on my knee,
I asked him to lend me fifty pence,
But he borrowed a pound from me.

Oh, what a funny bug is lightning
bug;
His light is on the wrong end.
He never sees where he's going
But only where he's been.

A conscience is a kill-joy,
It takes away the fun
You had in doing something
You shouldn't oughta done.

Willie saw some dynamite,
Couldn't understand it quite.
Curiosity never pays,
It rained Willie seven days.

I know that
I shall never see
A rocket soar
With cowardly me.

Sue frowned and called me Mr.
Because for sport I kr.
And so for spite,
That very night,
This Mr. kr. sr.

Dollar for dollar,
Pound for Pound,
Money's nice
To have around.

Swans sing before they die,
'Twere no bad thing
Should certain persons die
Before they sing.

Beneath this weeping willow tree
Lies Edward Everett Greer;
Who by another hunter was
Mistaken for a deer.

Willie, writing on the bed,
Spilled some ink on Mother's spread.
"Mum," he said, when she came back,
"It will dye a lovely black."

God rest ye merry gentlemen,
Let nothing you dismay.
Unless it's all the Christmas bills
Your wife told you to pay.

Mary had a little car,
She drove it day and night,
But every time she signalled left,
Her little car turned right.

I envy you, dear lightning bug,
You worry not a bit,
For when you see a traffic cop,
You know your tail light's lit.

The saddest words of tongue or pen
May be perhaps, "It might have been,"
But the sweetest words *we* ever knew
Are, "Son, here's twenty pounds for you."

Mary had a little lamb,
A pizza and some prunes,
A glass of milk, a piece of pie,
And then some macaroons;
It made the happy waiters grin
To see her order so;
And when they carried Mary out,
Her face was white as snow.

He rocked the boat,
Did Ezra Shank,
These bubbles mark
    O
    O
    O
    O
Where Ezra sank.

Willie, at a passing gent,
Threw a batch of wet cement,
Shouting, "Wait until you dry,
Then you'll be a real hard guy!"

Under the spreading chestnut tree
The smith works like the deuce.
For now he's selling gas and oil,
Hot dogs and orange juice.

Ruth rode my motorcycle
On the seat in back of me;
I took a bump at fifty-five,
And rode on Ruthlessly.

I wish I were a kangaroo,
Despite their funny stances;
I'd have a place to put the junk
My girl brings to the dances.

Willie, when the wind was strong,
Flew his kite all morning long.
"Look!" he cried. "Just see it dance!
I made it out of Papa's pants."

I love to stand upon my head
And think of things sublime.
Until my mother interrupts
And says it's dinner time.

Willie, hitting at a ball,
Lined one down the school-house hall.
Through his door came Dr. Hill.
Thirteen teeth are missing still!

When it freezes and blows,
Take care of your nose,
So it won't get froze.
And wrap up your toes
In warm woollen hose,
And so, I suppose,
Even though it ain't prose,
This verse still shows
The effects of cold snows.

Yesterday upon the stair,
I saw a man who wasn't there,
He wasn't there again today,
My gosh, I wish he'd go away.

It's easy enough to be happy
When the sun shines on the town,
But the man worthwhile
Is the man who can smile
When his trousers are falling down.

Be kind to the moose
He may be of some use,
For hanging your hat
Or something like that.

I always fly
Into a rage
When someone mutters,
"Act your age!"

With a sharp doo-dah I'd like to poke
The everlasting lout,
Who, when I'm telling my best joke,
Gets up and moves about.

CRAZY CROSSES

What do you get if you cross a termite with a house?
An exterminator.

What do you get if you cross a vulture with a little grass shack?
A scavenger hut.

What do you get if you cross a fawn with a hornet?
Bambee.

What do you get if you cross a mosquito and an elephant?
I don't know, but if it bites you, you're in real trouble.

What do you get if you cross a foot and a rocket?
Mistletoe.

What do you get if you cross a hummingbird with a bell?
A humdinger.

What do you get if you cross Telly Savalas and a pool table?
A billiard bald.

What do you get if you cross a tiger with a needle?
Pin stripes.

What do you get if you cross a skeleton with a great detective?
Sherlock Bones.

What do you get if you cross a duck hunter with a parrot?
A bird that says, "Polly wants a quacker."

What do you get if you cross a rattlesnake with a doughnut?
A snake that rattles and rolls.

What do you get if you cross the Green Giant with Robin Hood?
A Ho-Bow

What do you get if you cross an ancient Greek superhero with a sheep?
Hercufleece!

What do you get if you cross a penguin and a zebra?
An animal in a striped suit.

What do you get if you cross a steer with a tadpole?
A bullfrog.

What do you get if you cross a hungry cat with a canary?
A cat that's not hungry anymore.

What do you get if you cross a match with a mosquito?
A firebug that burns you up when it bites you.

What do you get if you cross a canary and a mole?
A miner bird.

What do you get if you cross a ham and a karate expert?

Pork chops.

What do you get if you cross a kitten and a sapling?

A pussy willow.

What do you get if you cross a pig and a cactus?

A porkerpine.

What do you get when you cross a poodle and a cuckoo clock?

A watch dog.

What do you get if you cross an envelope with a homing pigeon?

A letter that comes back to you everytime you mail it.

What do you get if you cross an elephant with a spider?

I don't know, but when it crawls on your ceiling, the roof collapses!

What do you get if you cross a man-eating tiger and a dog?

An animal that eats people and buries their bones.

What do you get if you cross Satan with a pig?

Deviled ham.

What do you get if you cross two insects and a rabbit?

Bugs Bunny.

What do you get when you cross a pig with a porcupine?

Bacon and pegs.

What do you get if you cross an elephant and a cactus?
   The biggest porcupine in the world.

What do you get if you cross a steer and Niagara
Falls?
   A water buffalo.

What do you get if you cross a frog with an elephant?
   *I don't know, but it takes a lot of flies to satisfy
its appetite.*

What do you get if you cross a pig and a turkey?
   *An animal that makes a hog of himself at
Christmas!*

What do you get if you cross an elephant with a swift
football striker?
   I don't know, but it sure scores a lot of goals.

What do you get if you cross a cat with a cactus?
   *An animal that gives you a pain whenever it rubs
against your leg.*

YOU TELL 'EM

You tell 'em, Aviator,
You're a high flyer.

You tell 'em, Banana,
You've been skinned.

You tell 'em, Bean,
She's stringing you.

You tell 'em, Baldy,
You're smooth.

You tell 'em, Calendar,
You've got lots of dates.

You tell 'em, Cat,
That's what you're fur.

You tell 'em, Cashier,
I'm a poor teller.

You tell 'em, Clock,
You've got the time.

You tell 'em, Doctor,
You've got the patience.

You tell 'em, Teacher,
You've got the class.

You tell 'em, Operator,
You've got their number.

You tell 'em, Dentist,
You've got the pull.

You tell 'em, Horse,
You carry a tale.

You tell 'em, Simon,
I'll Legree.

You tell 'em, Skyscraper,
You have more than one storey.

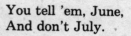

You tell 'em, Hunter,
I'm game.

You tell 'em, June,
And don't July.

MONSTER MADNESS

Why did the cyclops have to close his school?
Because he only had one pupil.

What do vampires hate to have for dinner?
T-Bone Stakes.

What business is King Kong in?
Monkey business.

What do ghosts ride at an amusement park?
The roller ghoster.

What has one wheel and gets ten miles to a gallon of plasma?
A vampire on a unicycle.

What's hairy, has fangs, and is four feet tall?
An eight-foot werewolf bending over to tie his shoe.

Why did the vampire walk around in his pyjamas?
Because he didn't have a batrobe.

Why does Frankenstein look so stiff when he walks?
Because Dr. Frankenstein's wife put too much starch in his underwear.

What do you call it when a ghost makes a mistake?
A Booo-Booo!

What did Santa Claus bring the Egyptian Pharaoh at Christmas?
A gift-wrapped mummy.

Where do spooks mail their letters?
At the ghost post office.

Why did the Frankenstein monster go to a psychiatrist?
Because he thought one of his screws was loose.

What did the father ghost tell the little ghost?
"Don't spook til you're spooken to."

What's green, likes peanuts, and weighs two tons?
A little green elephant from Mars.

What's eight feet tall, patriotic, and flies a kite in a rain storm?
Benjamin Frankenstein.

How do you stop a werewolf from attacking you?
Throw a stick and yell, "Fetch Boy!"

Why did the witch fail in school?
Because she couldn't spell.

How did the fire-breathing dragon burn his fingers?
He had a cold, and every time, he sneezed he covered his mouth with his hand.

Why didn't the spirit buy a lottery ticket?
Because he didn't think he had a ghost of a chance of winning.

Why did King Kong join the Marines?
Because he wanted to learn about gorilla warfare.

What was the first place Dracula visited when he went to New York?
The Vampire State Building.

How did the warlock make the beautiful princess fall in love with him?
He charmed her.

When Dracula plays baseball, what does he use when it's his turn to hit?
A vampire bat.

"Did you hear about the poor mad scientist who couldn't afford to pay his electric bill?"
"No. What about him?"
"He had to fly a kite during a thunderstorm and tie it to his monster."

"When I die, I don't want to come back as a ghost. I want to come back as a mattress."
"Why?"
"So I can lie in bed all day."

Oliver: Mr. Ghost, how much will you charge to haunt my girlfriend's father?
Mr. Ghost: For £10 I promise to scare him out of his wits.
Oliver: Well, here, take £5. He's only a half-wit.

Did you hear about the little ghost who was so small that he couldn't fit in a sheet so he had to wear a pillowcase?

Why do witches ride broomsticks from Lands End to John O'Groats.
Because the extension cords on their vacuum cleaners aren't long enough.

What did the little ghost say to Miss America?
"Gee, you're boo-tiful!"

Why was the Egyptian pharaoh so sad?
Because he thought he'd lost his mummy.

Where does a vampire keep his savings?
In a blood bank.

Who's a vampire's worst enemy?
Mr. Tooth Decay.

What does the invisible man put on his face before he goes to bed at night?
Vanishing Cream.

Why did the crazy vampire try out with the New York Yankees?
He thought he was a baseball bat.

Girl: Want to hear an old Transylvanian saying?
Boy: *Sure. What is it?*
Girl: A clove of garlic a day keeps the vampires away.

Do devils have bad tempers?
Yes. They're always hot under the collar.

Werewolf: Last night I had that new young couple that
just moved in down the road for dinner at my
house.
Dracula: *Were they enjoyable?*
Werewolf: They were more than enjoyable; they were
delicious.

What is the most dangerous job in Transylvania?
*Being a dog catcher on nights when the moon is
full.*

How do you make a Big Mac monster burger?
*You put two people patties, special sauce, lettuce,
cheese, pickles, and onions on a sesame seed bun.*

What's the second most dangerous job in Transylvania?
Being Count Dracula's dentist!

How can you tell if a vampire is insane?
If he's insane, he'll have bats in his belfry.

What does the Abominable Snowman have for lunch?
Cold cuts.

Did you hear about the midget witch who was so small
that she flew around on a whisk broom?

WHY DON'T THEY ALSO INVENT....

Spaghetti a hundred feet long — for people who like their dinner in one long slurp.

Silent electric mixers — for having a quiet get-together.

Soapy erasers — for cleaning paper plates.

A rubber postage stamp — for posting bouncing cheques.

A bag of salted butter — for people who hate popcorn at the cinema.

A magical password — for opening cans.

A paddle with holes in it — for canoeists who aren't in a hurry.

A rake with no teeth — for raking a garden with no trees.

A dry canal — for barges with wheels.

Artificial lambs — for sheep dogs that live in the city.

Dry lakes — for fish who are afraid of the water.

Vitamin-fortified soda pop — for babies who don't like milk.

Little pogo sticks — for tired grasshoppers.

A "smart" pill you can take the night before a test — so you can go to the pictures instead of studying.

Shoes with stainless steel soles and heels — so they never wear out.

Clothes with adjustable sizes you can still wear — if you gain or lose weight.

A crash helmet made out of foam rubber — for people who fall out of bed.

Ice that never melts — so people can go skating in the summer.

Golf holes that expand — so your ball always reaches them in one stroke.

Dog collars — for fleas.

A slot machine that registers a jackpot every time — for poor people to play.

A bath with holes in it — for kids who have to get washed before going to bed, but hate to take baths.

A scale with no numbers on it — for people who hate to see that they're overweight.

A gun that fires cotton-wool bullets — for hunters who are animal lovers.

A dictionary with blank pages — for people who know it all.

Overcoats for birds — so they can stay warm without flying south for the winter.

Postage stamps with glue in assorted fruit flavours — for tasty licks.

Trousers with lead-lined turn-ups — to keep people who are full of hot air from floating away.

No-drip soup spoons — for sloppy eaters.

A bank that loans money to kids — so they don't have to ask their parents for advances in their pocket money.

Robot shoes that dance by themselves when music comes on — so people never have to take dancing lessons.

A bowling ball made out of foam rubber — for weak bowlers.

Bad school reports that automatically self-destruct on the way home.

Telephones in the shape of bowlers — for people who like to talk through their hats.

A remote control lawn mower — that doesn't have to be pushed.

TV alarm clocks that ring when it's time to go to sleep — for people who doze off while watching the late show.

Hand-to-hand combat courses for birds — so they can defend themselves against cats who try to catch them.

Bananas and oranges with edible skins — so you don't have to peel them.

Maple trees with taps in them — so it's easier to remove the syrup.

Inexpensive disposable cars that can be thrown away when something goes wrong with them — so you don't have to pay car repair bills.

Envelopes with wings that fly to the post office — so you don't have to go out to post them.

A tongue depressor — for looking into sick shoes.

A bottle with a top shaped like a hat — for people who want a nightcap.

Transparent shades — for people who don't want privacy.

Spinach ripple ice cream — for health-conscious people.

Mid-ocean airfields — for flying fish.

Little tiny motorboats — for ducks who can't swim.

A clock with wings — to make time fly.

A book with no printing — for people who hate to read.

A pickled onion pie — for people who don't like sweet desserts.

An egg with no shell — for people who hate to break things.

A camel with three humps — so he'll always have a spare.

Pre-drilled apples — for worms who hate to dig.

A flute with no holes — for pipers who can't play.

A calendar with December missing — for saving the lives of millions of turkeys.

Cast iron bed springs — for people who like a firm mattress.

Flashcandles for cameras — for snapping romantic pictures.

A cloth pound — so it will shrink in proportion to its actual value.

Cigarettes made out of shredded rubbish — to discourage people from smoking.

A diamond that sends out a radio signal — so it can be tracked down in case it's stolen.

Furniture that repels dust — so it never has to be dusted.

A magic wallet that automatically refills itself with money when it's empty — for people who spend more than they earn.

One-way windows in houses — so you can see out, but no one can see in.

Kites with wings — for you to fly when there's no wind.

Toupées made out of grass — for bald spots in the lawn.

Junior credit cards — for kids who want to buy toys, ice cream, and sweets when they're short of cash.

A back garden bird shower — for birds who don't like to take baths.

Library books with robot legs and computerized brains — so they can automatically return themselves to the library when they're due.

A dentist drill that hums instead of making that horrible noise.

Toupées made out of feathers — for bald eagles.

A boomerang ball that returns to you after you throw it — so you can play catch when no one else is around.

Medicine that really tastes good — so you don't mind taking it.

Toothpicks made out of steel — for beavers who get wood stuck in their teeth.

A pill you can take that changes you overnight from a 7-stone weakling into a 15-stone muscleman.

Trousers with pillows sewn in the back pockets — for clumsy people who like to ice skate and roller skate.

Balsa wood bricks — for karate experts with tender hands, to break in half.

An alarm clock that rings on relatives' birthdays — to remind you to buy a gift.

Pencils with indestructible points — so they never break off and never have to be sharpened.

Leaves that self-destruct when they hit the ground — so you don't have to rake them up in the Autumn.

An aeroplane that runs on rails — for people who are afraid to fly.

A newspaper that prints only good news.

A machine for making a ring in the bath — for kids who want their mothers to think they took a bath.

A kettle that hums — so you don't have to listen to shrill whistles.

An oven that refrigerates — for cooking a cold supper.

Giant deep freezers — for storing igloos during the summer.

Chocolate flavoured Brussel sprouts — for making vegetables taste better.

Flat hair curlers — for girls who wear their hair straight.

A bottomless biscuit tin — for biscuit monsters with bottomless stomachs.

Biscuits with handles — for tidy dunkers.

A magic postbox that changes bills into cheques.

Teacher's Pests

Teacher: Judy, please spell "banana."
Judy: B-a-n-a-n-a — I know how to spell it, but I don't know when to stop.

Teacher: What great event happened in 1809?
James: Abraham Lincoln was born.
Teacher: Correct. And what great event happened in 1812?
James: Abraham Lincoln had his third birthday.

Teacher: Arthur, if you had three apples and ate one, how many would you have?
Arthur: Three.
Teacher: Three?
Arthur: Yes. Two outside and one inside.

Teacher: If you stood with your back to the north and faced due south, what would be on your left hand?
Davey: Fingers.

Teacher: If you add 500, 391, 38, 162, and 17, then divide by 39 what would you get?
Lisa: The wrong answer.

Teacher: Oscar, if you had five pieces of candy, and Joey asked you for one, how many pieces would you have left?
Oscar: Five.

Band Student: Our high school orchestra played Beethoven last night.
Athlete: Who won?

Teacher: Birds, though small, are remarkable creatures.
For example, what can a bird do that I can't do?
Eager Earl: Take a bath in a saucer.

Teacher: How did you get that horrible swelling on
your nose?
Smart Scott: I bent over to smell a brose.
Teacher: There's no "b" in rose.
Smart Scott: There was in this one.

American Teacher: Who was the first man?
American Boy: George Washington.
American Teacher: No, it was Adam.
*American Boy: Oh, I didn't know you were
including foreigners.*

Teacher: If I lay one egg on this chair and two on the
table, how many will I have all together?
Sylvester: Personally, I don't believe you can do it.

"What are the three words most often used by
students?"
"*I don't know.*"
"That's correct."

In school, they nicknamed me "Corns" because I'm
always at the foot of my class.

Little Jimmy came home from his first day at school
and told his mother he was never going back.
"What's the use of school?" he said. "I can't read and
I can't write, and the teacher won't let me talk."

Jeff: Today, on the school bus, a little boy fell off his
seat, and everybody laughed except me.
Teacher: Who was the little boy?
Jeff: Me.

Teacher: Yes, what is it?
Failing Student: *I don't want to frighten you, but Dad said that if I don't get better grades, someone's going to get a spanking.*

Teacher: *Do you know why you make such poor grades?*
Mortimer: *I can't think.*
Teacher: That's right.

Teacher: Spell "cattle."
Suzie: *C-A-T-T-T-L-E.*
Teacher: Leave out one of the t's.
Suzie: *Which one?*

Teacher: It's the law of gravity that keeps us from falling off the earth.
Silly Sally: *What kept us from falling off before the law was passed?*

Teacher: If I gave you two apples and told you to give one to your brother, would you give him the little one or the big one?
Ricky: *Do you mean my little brother or my big brother?*

The teacher was talking about Dumb Denny. "He has a mind exactly like a blotter," she said. "He soaks up everything he hears, but he gets it all backwards."

"I won a prize in nursery school today," announced Little Julie. "The teacher asked us how many legs a dog has and I said three."
"*You won a prize for saying a dog has three legs?*" said her father. "*How did you do that?*"
"Well I came the closest."

Teacher: How do you spell weather?
Aubrey: *W-E-O-T-H-E-R.*
Teacher: Terrible! That's the worst spell of weather we've had in a long time.

A mathematics professor was run over by a truck. *"Did you get the licence number?" asked the policeman.*

"Well, not exactly," the professor replied, "but I do remember noticing that if it was doubled and then multiplied by itself, the square root of the product was the original number with the integers reversed."

Teacher: Now, class, are there any questions?
Dizzy Izzy: Yes. Where do those words go when you rub them off the blackboard?

Teacher: Name four animals that belong to the cat family.
Little Lena: The mummy cat, the daddy cat, and two kittens.

The teacher had asked her pupils to name the 11 greatest Britains. All the students had turned their papers except Jimmy.
"Can't you finish your list, Jimmy?"
"Not yet," replied Jimmy. "I'm still undecided about the goalkeeper."

Teacher: Albert, tell us where the English Channel is.
Albert: I don't know. I can't find it on my TV set.

"As we have learned," said the teacher, "the former ruler of Russia was called the Czar. His wife was called the Czarina. Now, who can tell me what the Czar's children were called?"
A voice from the rear of the class responded, "Czardines."

Chemistry Teacher: What can you tell me about nitrates?
Cute Carol: Well, I think they're cheaper than day rates.

Teacher: Small Sam, why are you so late this morning?
Small Sam: *Every step I took, I slipped back two.*
Teacher: At that rate, you wouldn't be here now.
Small Sam: *Oh, I turned around and walked the
other way.*

Teacher: We know that heat causes an object to
expand and cold causes it to contract. Now, can
anyone give me a good example?
Smart Scott: *Well, in the summer the days are long,
and in the winter the days are short.*

Curious Chris: Is a chicken big enough to eat when it's
three weeks old?
Teacher: *Of course not.*
Curious Chris: Then how does it manage to live?

Little Willie finished his breakfast, then rushed off to
school without washing his face.
His teacher looked at him, frowned and said, "Willie,
you didn't wash your face. What would you say if I
came to school with egg and jam all over my face?"
"Nothing," replied Willie. "I'd be too polite."

Teacher: Which month has twenty-eight days?
Eager Earl: *They all do.*

"Name two pronouns."
"Who, me?"
"Correct."

Teacher: At your age, I could name all the Kings &
Queens — and in the proper order.
Mortimer: *Sure, but in those days there were only
three or four of them.*

"Iceland is about the same size as Siam," said the
teacher.
*"Iceland," wrote Charlie on his test paper, "is
about the same size as my teacher."*

84

Albert: I don't have a pencil to take this exam.
*Teacher: What would you think of a soldier who
went to battle without a gun?*
Albert: I'd think he was an officer.

Teacher: What's wrong with this sentence, "The horse
and cow is in the field."?
Polite Perry: Ladies should come first.

School Superintendent: Are there any unusual students
in your class?
Teacher: Yes — three of them have good manners.

Teacher: What's usually used as a conductor of
electricity?
Orville: Why - er....
Teacher: Correct, wire. Now tell me, what is the unit of
electrical power?
Orville: The what?
Teacher: That's absolutely right. The watt.

Teacher: How do you spell Mississippi?
Small Sam: The river or the state?

When I was in school, I was the teacher's pet. She
couldn't afford a dog.

Teacher: Charlie, can you define the system of checks
and balances?
Charlie: Sure, we have that in our family.
Teacher: How do you mean?
Charlie: I have the vote and dad has the veto.

Teacher: Vicki, what's a leading cause of dry skin?
Vicki: Towels.

Teacher: Lavinia, where would you find the State Department, the Department of Education, and the Department of Defence?
Lavinia: In a department store.

Teacher: What animal is satisfied with the least nourishment?
Student: Moths. They eat nothing but holes.

Teacher: Our subject in Social Studies today is overcrowding. Freddie can you give an example of overcrowding?
Freddie: Rub-a-dub-dub, three men in a tub.

Teacher: Benny, can you explain inflation?
Benny: Sure. Every time my dad pays the bills, he blows up. That's inflation.

Teacher: Everyone knows we should conserve energy. Billy, name one way we can do that.
Billy: By staying in bed all day.

Teacher: Sally, what's the first thing you should do with a barrel of crude oil?
Sally: Teach it some manners.

Teacher: Betty, do you know the tenth President of the United States?
Betty: No, we've never been introduced.

Teacher: Peggy, what's the difference between the sun and the moon?
Peggy: They're as different as night and day.

Teacher: Harvey, do you ever have trouble making decisions?
Harvey: Well...yes and no.

Teacher: Larry, define procrastination.
Larry: *Teacher, is it all right if I answer that question tomorrow?*

Teacher: Dora, can you define classical music?
Dora: *Sure. Anything without an electric guitar.*

Teacher: Albert, if you insist on talking, I'll have to send you to the principal's office.
Albert: *Oh, does the principal want somebody to talk to?*

Teacher: Tommy, what are you drawing?
Tommy: *A picture of God.*
Teacher: But, Tommy, nobody knows how God looks.
Tommy: *They will when I get this picture done.*

Teacher: Lester, I think you should take something for that cold.
Lester: *Oh, good. I'll take the rest of the week off.*

Teacher: Carol, who do you think is responsible for the high cost of electricity?
Carol: *The man who comes to read the meter.*

Teacher: William, please complete this sentence... "If at first you don't succeed..."
William: *Forget the whole thing and go fishing.*

Teacher: Tommy, if you don't know where the Appalachians are, I am going to have to keep you after school.
Tommy: *Honest, teacher, I didn't take them.*

Teacher: Robert, are you paying attention?
Robert: *Yes, teacher.*
Teacher: Then why is your nose buried in that comic?
Robert: *I'm paying attention to the comic.*

Teacher: Tomorrow, I want every student to write a two-page essay on a subject of your own choice. Jenny, what are you going to write about?

Jenny: *About how much I hate to write essays.*

Teacher: Sylvester, what's the definition of ignorance?

Sylvester: *I don't know.*

Teacher: Joey, your behaviour is terrible! How many more times am I going to have to keep you in after school?

Joey: *97.*

Teacher: 97?

Joey: *Yeah. That's how may days are left until the summer holiday.*

Teacher: Mark, what's the one way a person can show that he's a good loser?

Mark: *By not punching the winner on the nose.*

Teacher: Lucy, where are you going on your summer holiday?

Lucy: *Iceland.*

Teacher: That's interesting. Why did you choose Iceland?

Lucy: *We want to see it before it melts.*

Teacher: Everybody knows that Alexander Graham Bell invented the telephone. Stacy, what did his assistant, Mr. Watson do?
Stacy: *He sent out the phone bills.*

Teacher: Nancy, describe the Battle of the Bulge.
Nancy: *My mother when she goes on a diet.*

Teacher: Brenda, why don't you want to come on our field trip to study insects?
Brenda: *Because they bug me.*

Teacher: Patrick, you should know the answer to this one... What happens to a person when he kisses the Blarney Stone?
Patrick: *He gets cold, dirty lips.*

Teacher: Jose, when was the great depression?
Jose: *Last week when I got my school report.*

Teacher: Zeke, what, besides a supersonic jet, goes faster than the speed of sound?
Zeke: *My Aunt Gladys when she talks.*

Why Don't They Invent?

Neon thumbs — for night hitchhikers.

An automobile without a horn - for people who don't give a hoot.

A stepladder without steps on it — for washing basement windows.

An alarm clock with half a bell — for waking only one of two people who sleep in the same room.

Another alarm clock without a bell — for people who are retired.

A cookbook with nothing in it but blank pages — for writing down the names and addresses of good restaurants.

A fish hook with a camera on it — to take pictures of the one that got away.

A cuckoo clock where the cuckoo comes out and asks, "What time is it?"

A lamp with no bulbs — for people who like to sit in the dark.

A shotgun with one barrel on top of the other, instead of side by side — for shooting ducks that happen to be flying piggy-back.

A motorized fish bowl — so you can take your pet fish for a walk in the park.

A hammer with a head made of foam rubber — for clumsy carpenters who are always hitting their thumbs.

A wind-up babysitter robot — so you will have someone to stay at home and watch your baby brother on Saturday night while you go out with your friends.

An "UNWELCOME" mat to put in front of your door — to discourage peddlers and debt collectors.

Invisible braces — so people can have their teeth straightened without looking silly.

A combination oven and television set — so you can heat TV dinners while you watch your favourite programme.

A talking digital watch that tells you where you're supposed to be at what time — so you're never late for anything.

Flower pots with built in sprinkler systems — so you never have to water your plants.

A bicycle that pedals itself up steep hills.

Dustbins with legs — so they can take themselves out and let you sleep.

A perfumed bookmark. If it slips down into the book, just sniff along the edge till you find your place.

A telephone that won't ring until you're standing right by it.

An upside-down lighthouse — for submarines.

A cup made of everlasting coffee-flavoured plastic. Simply fill with hot water, cream and sugar.

Rubber trains. They save space by curling up in the shed.

A wristwatch with a whistle on it — in case someone comes up to you and says, "Hey! Have you got a wristwatch with a whistle on it?"

Confatty — for throwing at stout people when they get married.

Toothless combs — for people who don't have any hair.

A bridge that goes halfway across a river, then turns around and comes back — for people who change their minds.

Newspapers printed on cellophane — so wives can see their husbands at the breakfast table.

A perfume that drives bankers crazy. It smells like money.

A dog food that tastes like a postman's leg.

A long knife that can cut four loaves of bread at the same time. It's called a four-loaf cleaver.

A quick parking car. You just press a button on the dashboard and the car folds up and hides itself in its own glove compartment.

A TV set twenty-three inches wide and only one inch high — for people who squint.

A hot dog ninety feet long — to take care of a whole row at the football match.

Books that come with book reports at the end — so you don't have to do all those reading assignments.

Plastic song books — for people who like to sing in the shower.

A new kind of tranquiliser. It doesn't relax you. It just makes you contented to be tense.

Cellophane shirts — for people who have to watch their waistlines.

An invisible dog collar — for people who have an invisible dog.

A birdcage forty feet high — to keep your thirty-nine-foot-tall canary in.

A mousetrap that just screams, "Get outta here!" instead of snapping shut — for people with tender hearts.

A typewriter that has no A, E, I, O, or U on it — for people who hate vowels.

Motorised roller skates — for people who can't afford to buy cars or motorcycles.

A rubber toothpick that bends instead of breaking when you use it.

Shirts and blouses with boards sewn into the seams — for people with poor posture.

Diet gravy — for people who have to lose weight, but hate plain mashed potatoes.

A pair of robot slippers that will fetch your pet dog.

A shower button that automatically adjusts the water to the correct temperature when you press it.

A robot pet dog that never has to be brushed, fed, or walked.

A machine that converts polluted water into soda pop.

A record album that is absolutely scratch-proof.

Belts that automatically loosen themselves when you overeat.

Shirt collars made out of iron — for people who work nights and live in Transylvania.

Talking comic books — for little kids who haven't learnt how to read yet.

A new candy that tastes good and doesn't give you cavities.

Moving pavements — so you can shop all day and never get tired of walking.

A tennis net that automatically lowers itself after a match — so you can easily jump over it.

Neckties that tie themselves around your neck.

Pizza-flavoured bubble gum.

Shirts with buttons that grow back — if the original ones fall off.

A talking breakfast cereal that tells you the answers to exam questions — so you don't have to study for an exam the night before.

Tomato sauce that you can fingerpaint onto spaghetti — so you can play with your food before you eat it.

A diary that self-destructs — if anyone other than you tries to read it.

Back pants' pockets with combination locks on them — to discourage pickpockets.

A car with automatic pilot — for people who fall asleep behind the wheel.

Chocolate covered spinach — for kids who love sweets and hate to eat what's good for them.

A combination fly swatter-tennis racket — so you can swat flies and practice your serve at the same time.

Pens that write only the right answers to exam questions.

Glasses with no glass in them — for people with good eyes who like to look studious.

A car with a built-in direction finder — for people who always take the wrong turn and get lost.

Murder mysteries that have the last chapter first — for people who can't wait to find out who did it.

Candy-coated soda cans that people can eat — so they
don't litter the roads.

A shoe with laces that tie themselves.

Pencils without erasers — for people who never make
mistakes.

A boomerang arrow — for hunters who always miss
their target and lose their arrows.

An inexpensive robot that will do homework.

A no-drip ice cream cone.

A clock that runs very fast in the winter and very, very
slow in the summer.

Capsules that grow into plastic flowers when you
water them.

A basketball that goes into the basket everytime
you shoot it.

A baseball bat that hits a home run on every pitch.

Disposable clothes that can be thrown away when they
get dirty — so you don't have to wash them.

A bed with robot arms that makes itself in the
morning.

A mirror that makes you look good first thing in
the morning.

A bed with a built-in catapult that shoots you out of
bed — if you don't get up when the alarm goes off.

A mouth organ that plays itself — for people who'd
like to be musicians but have no talent.

A camera that takes only good pictures of people.

A dictionary computer that tells you how to spell
words — so you don't have to look them up.

A combination letterbox-waste disposal that chews up
junk mail and bills.

Gift-wrapped empty boxes — to give as presents to
people who say, "I don't need anything."

A fork that bends if you put too much food on it — for
people who are on diets.

A television set that automatically shuts itself off and
on before and after the commercials.

Reusable bubble gum that never has to be thrown
away.

School buses that automatically head for the town pool
— for kids who hate to go to school on hot June
days.

A car that runs on pollutants instead of making them.

INSULTS!

He's so lazy that waking up in the morning makes
   him tired.

The only exercise he gets is from stretching when
   he yawns.

You have a pretty little head. For a head, it's pretty
   little.

Is that your nose, or are you eating a banana?

His I.Q. is so low that he doesn't even know what
   I.Q. stands for.

Is that your head, or are you carrying a watermelon
   on your shoulders.

I can't take anything away from her I.Q. How can
   you subtract from zero.

He's such a blockhead that his mother took out wood
   worm insurance on his brain.

The last time he went to the zoo, attendants chased
   him for two hours. They thought he'd escaped
   from one of the cages.

Hey! Do you want to see something funny? Look in a mirror.

You're so out of shape, the government would pay you *not* to donate your body to science.

Everyone thought he was a marvel of modern science until they discovered he was a boy instead of a talking chimp.

If she had a body to match her face, her parents could enter her in the Derby.

If stupidity was gold, you'd be Fort Knox.

I dreamed about you last night. My mother told me if I had a snack before I went to bed, I'd have nightmares.

I hear you're famous. A costume company is using your face as a model for its Halloween masks.

He's very useful at picnics. He keeps the flies away from the food.

You're so stupid that when you get a brainstorm, it's nothing but a drizzle.

I just searched your family tree and found out you're the sap.

You're so weak, you couldn't beat eggs.

She's got a soft heart and a head to match.

The only time you have something on your mind is when you wear a hat.

You're so weak, you couldn't whip cream.

I wouldn't say he's a blockhead, but a flock of woodpeckers follows him wherever he goes.

Did you know a movie producer wants to buy the rights to your life story? He figures it will make a great horror picture.

The only dates she gets are blind dates. As long as the guys can't see her face, they don't get sick to their stomachs.

What did Santa Claus bring you for Christmas last year — a flea collar and a rubber bone?

You're a very brave person. If I had a face like yours, I'd be ashamed to come out of the house.

He's so stupid, his mother had to tatoo his name on his arm so he wouldn't forget who he is.

He stopped singing to his plants because his breath made them wilt.

You certainly do look like a big movie star — the Frankenstein monster.

If you stood on a corner thumbing a ride, the only person who'd pick you up would be the dog catcher.

Looking at your face makes me wish I was old enough to drink.

I've seen better bodies used on cars.

When he goes to the zoo, the monkeys throw peanuts at *him*.

Kissing a porcupine would be less painful than kissing you.

The last time she went to the circus, an elephant asked her for a date.

The circus just came to town. Why don't you talk to the ringmaster about getting a job? I hear they're in the market for a trained hippo.

Next to you, Moby Dick looks like a sardine.

Your face keeps hospitals in business — people take one look at you and get sick.

You've got a bionic body, but your brain is rusty.

It's a good thing Buffalo Bill isn't around today, or your life would be in real danger.

Tell me, how did you manage to live through last Christmas?

If you stood on a corner, the only person who'd pick you up would be the dustman.

You're so thick, if you wrote a novel it would be a best smeller.

The last time I saw ears as big as yours, they were on corn.

If they made you into a six-million-dollar person, you'd be the first bionic blimp.

You look like the "before" model in a "before and after" nose-job commercial.

The last time she went to the monkey cage at the zoo, she got three proposals of marriage.

They say everyone in the world has a double and now I know it's true. I saw your double last week. His name was Kongo and he was in the gorilla cage at the zoo.

You're so weak, you have to take vitamins in order to get enough strength to bend licquorice.

I hear your boyfriend won't be able to see you anymore. From now on Dr. Frankenstein is keeping his monster chained up at night.

You've got about as many muscles as an under-nourished worm.

If you value your life, hide quick! Here comes the dog catcher.

Did you forget to take off your halloween mask, or do you really look like that?

The last time he went to the circus, the sideshow freaks laughed at *him.*

That's some shape you've got. I've seen better figures on toothpicks.

You don't have enough brains in your head to fill a thimble.

I'd go out with you, but it's against my religion to date chimpanzees.

With her body, she could pose for the centrefold — in Popular Mechanics.

A BUNCH OF BONERS

Armadillo is the Spanish Navy that defeated the Duke of Wellington.

Monsoon is French for Mister.

Flora and Fauna were the names of Siamese twins.

Davy Jones was a famous engineer.

Thin silk material used for making ladies underwear is called Crepe Suzette.

Telepathy is a code invented by Morse.

Karl Marx is one of the Marx Brothers.

Philatelists were a race of people who lived in Biblical times.

Alma Mater was a famous opera singer

Daniel Boone was born in a log cabin he built himself.

Pate de foi gras is an outdoor circus held every year in New Orleans.

An Indian baby is called a caboose.

The Golden Rule is that the man who first finds gold gets to keep it.

Antimony is money you inherit from your mother's sister.

History calls people Romans because they never stayed in one place very long.

A tambourine is a curved club which can be hurled so that it will come back near the place from which it was thrown.

Cleopatra wore beautiful open-toed scandals.

A flying buttress is a lady butler on an aeroplane.

The earth resolves around the sun once a year.

The mother of Abraham Lincoln died in infancy.

A pulmotor is a kind of car engine that pulls instead of pushing the car.

Bisquit Tortoni was the man who invented radios.

In many states of America murderers are put to
death by electrolysis.

Seniors are Spanish men.

Sailors are sometimes called squabs for short.

Sir Walter Raleigh is a historical figure because he
invented cigarettes.

A squire is a flat figure that has four equal sides.

My mother sings in the church choir and she also plays
the church gorgon.

The Iron Age was right before drip-dry clothes were
invented.

Sometimes we have scrabble eggs for breakfast.

Blood vessels are ships that carry blood overseas.

Dense foliage is dumb leaves.

Cyclamates are two people riding bicycles.

Piglets are small primitive natives who live in the jungle and hunt with blowguns.

Pheasants are poor people who live in small European villages.

Polygamy is when one pygmy marries another pygmy.

The man had drops of respiration on his forehead from working out in the hot sun.

Polka dots are what Polish people put at the ends of their sentences instead of full-stops.

My father says vulgarity is the spice of life.

Our city doesn't have a president, but we have a mare who works at the city hall.

A sturgeon is a doctor who performs operations.

Pasteur discovered a cure for rabbis.

A psalmist tells fortunes by looking at the lines on people's hands.

Pineapples grow on pine trees.

Every April 5th, my father pays Inca tax.

Germany is where germs were discovered.

Marco Polo is a famous man because he invented the sport of water polo.

Wyatt Burp and Wild Bill Hiccup were great western marshals.

If a whooping crane sneezes on a person, that person catches whooping cough.

Before people can become doctors, they have to take the hippopotamus oath.

An open shop is a factory with windows, and a closed shop is one with air-conditioning.

An executive is a man who puts murderers to death.

Peter Minuit invented a popular dance in Colonial times.

Robinson Crusoe was a great opera singer.

Voltaire invented electricity.

Archimedes helped Noah build his boat.

Marseillaise is a French dressing for salad.

Florence Nightingale is the name of a fancy female bird.

Flotsam and Jetsam were a famous radio comedy team.

A fjord is a foreign car.

An aviary is a hotel for aviators.

A pomegranate is a small, yappy dog.

Optimists are doctors who treat eyes.

A doggerel is a small puppy.

Equestrians are people who live on the equator.

Columbine was Columbus' wife.

The Merchant of Venice sold things from a canal boat.

A diva is a swimmer who jumps off the high board.

Crazy Answers

Why would a man in jail catch the measles?
So he could break out.

Why did Mother Flea look so sad?
Because all her children were going to the dogs.

If a burglar got into the cellar, would the coal chute?
No, but the kindlin' wood.

What did the apple tree say to the farmer?
"Why don't you stop picking on me."

What did the apple say to the pie?
"You've got some crust."

What did the rug say to the floor?
"Don't move — I've got you covered."

What did the first candle say to the second candle?
"Are you going out tonight?"

What did the big rose say to the little rose?
"Hi bud."

What did the mayonnaise say to the refrigerator?
"Close the door, I'm dressing."

What did the adding machine say to the bookkeeper?
"You can count on me."

What did the painter say to the wall?
"One more crack like that and I'll plaster you."

What did the big toe say to the little toe?
"Don't look now, but there's a big heel following us."

What four letters of the alphabet do you use to play hide and seek?
O-I-C-U.

What did the big frying pan say to the small frying pan?
"Hi ya, small fry."

Why was the drop of ink crying?
Because he heard his mum was in the pen and he didn't know how long the sentence would be.

MORE KNOCKKNOCKS

Knock knock.
Who's there?
 Imus
Imus who?
 Imus get out of this rain.

Knock knock.
Who's there?
 X.
X who?
 X-tra, X-tra, read all about it.

Knock knock.
Who's there?
 Harry.
Harry who?
 Harry up, it's cold out here.

Knock knock.
Who's there?
 Sandy.
Sandy who?
 Sandy Claus!

Knock knock.
Who's there?
 A herd.
A herd who?
 A herd you were home, so I came over!